The Roman and Greek Imprint: Shaping the Modern World

By

Michael Andrew Lambert Jr

Table of Contents

Introduction 5

Chapter 1: Foundations of Governance in Ancient Greece   11

- Comparative Analysis of Athenian and American Democracy **13**
- Philosophical Perspectives on Democracy **19**
- Governmental Structures of Athens and Sparta **25**

Chapter 2: Social Structures and Cultural Practices   33

- Contrasting Social Structures of Athens and Sparta **35**
- The Role of Religion in Greek Society and Culture **39**
- The Enduring Legacy of Ancient Greece on Western Civilization **45**

Chapter 3: The Greek Wars: From Preservation to Collapse   53

- The Greco-Persian Wars **55**
- Athens' Struggles During and After the Peloponnesian War **61**

Chapter 4: From Etruscan Roots to Roman Republic   69

- Uncovering Roman-Etruscan Connections **71**
- The Fall of the Roman Republic **75**
- Unraveling the Roman-Etruscan Connection **81**

Chapter 5: Comparative Strategies and Outcomes   87

- Comparative Analysis of Sparta and Rome **89**
- Cleopatra VII and the Roman Power Struggle **95**
- The Rome-Macedon Rivalry **101**

Chapter 6: Education, Slavery, and Gender Roles   109

- Evolution of Educational Practices **111**
- Comparative Analysis of Slavery and Women's Roles **115**

Chapter 7: Assimilation and Evolution   123

- From Greek Gods to Roman Rituals **125**
- Cultural Crossroads **129**

Chapter 8: The Modern Advantage   137

- The Modern Age **139**
- Enduring Legacies **145**

Conclusion   154

Bibliography   159

Introduction

The ancient civilizations of Greece and Rome are celebrated for their significant contributions to art, architecture, philosophy, and technology, leaving a lasting impression on the modern world. Even though thousands of years have passed since their decline, the legacies of these cultures still influence contemporary society in countless ways. This chapter explores the lasting effects of Greco-Roman culture on our lives today, emphasizing how their groundbreaking ideas and innovations have formed the basis for many elements of the world we live in.

The impact of ancient Greece and Rome is especially noticeable in art and architecture. Greek art, known for its focus on proportion, balance, and idealized forms, established timeless standards of beauty that continue to inspire modern artists. Renowned Greek sculptures and architectural masterpieces, like the Parthenon and the Venus de Milo, have significantly shaped Western artistic traditions. Meanwhile, Roman innovations in engineering and architecture, such as the use of concrete, arches, and vaulted ceilings, have influenced contemporary construction methods and continue to inspire modern architectural designs and public buildings.

The technological innovations from the Greco-Roman period have left a significant legacy. The Romans excelled in engineering, creating aqueducts, roads, and bridges that laid the foundation for today's infrastructure. Meanwhile, the Greeks made remarkable contributions to mathematics and science, with influential figures like Archimedes and Euclid shaping modern scientific practices and technological developments. These early advancements serve as the bedrock for current engineering and scientific progress.

Furthermore, the philosophy and literature of ancient Greece and Rome have greatly impacted modern intellectual thought. Philosophers such as Socrates, Plato, and Aristotle established essential principles in ethics, political theory, and epistemology, which continue to influence contemporary debates. Additionally, the literary works of Greek and Roman authors, including the epic narratives of Homer and Virgil, are still vital to modern storytelling and literary structures.

In this chapter, we will delve into the different facets of Greco-Roman influence, showcasing how their groundbreaking innovations and concepts have not only persisted over time but have also been reinterpreted and built upon in today's world. By looking closely at the lasting impact of Greco-Roman culture, we can uncover important lessons about how ancient accomplishments still enhance and shape our modern society.

Chapter 1

Foundations of Governance in Ancient Greece

Comparative Analysis of Athenian and American Democracy

Citizenship and Franchise

Back in ancient Athens, only free-born male Athenians over 18 could take part in the democratic process. Women, slaves, and metics were left out. In contrast, the United States is more inclusive, granting citizenship and voting rights to all individuals over 18, regardless of race, gender, or socio-economic background.

The Procedure to Make Laws

In ancient Athens, the main governing body was the Assembly (Ekklesia), where all qualified citizens had the right to participate. The Council of 500 (Boule) was responsible for setting the agenda for the Assembly and overseeing the implementation of its resolutions (Rothchild, 2007). On the other hand, the United States operates under a representative democracy model, where elected representatives in Congress (Senate and House of Representatives) introduce, discuss, and vote on legislation. This framework is intended to effectively govern a larger and more varied population by having representatives advocate for their constituents.

The Power of the Judiciary

Athenian democracy had these cool courts called Dikasteria. They were made up of big groups of regular people who were randomly chosen from the population.

These courts had the power to make legal decisions (Rothchild, 2007). This way, everyday citizens got to be directly involved in the justice system. In the U.S., things are a bit different. The judiciary is its own branch of government, and judges are either appointed or elected to interpret laws and make sure justice is served. This separation is meant to keep the legislative and executive branches in check.

Judicial Review

Judicial review in Athens was conducted by these large citizen juries, which could overturn decisions and hold officials accountable (Rothchild, 2007). In the U.S., judicial review is performed by courts, with the Supreme Court having the ultimate authority to invalidate laws and executive actions that are deemed unconstitutional.

Constraining the Power of Public Officials

Athenians had different methods to limit the authority of government officials. One of these was ostracism, which allowed citizens to vote and banish a potentially harmful individual for a decade (Rothchild, 2007). Moreover, officials were constantly monitored and could be held responsible through public trials. In the United States, the system of checks and balances between the executive, legislative, and judicial branches guarantees that no single branch becomes overly dominant. There are also impeachment procedures in place to remove officials who misuse their power.

To sum it up, Athenian democracy and the U.S. democratic system may have the same aim of empowering citizens and avoiding tyranny, but their approaches are shaped by their unique historical and cultural backgrounds. Athens embraced direct democracy, enabling its citizens to actively participate in decision-making, which was suitable for its smaller population. On the other hand, the U.S. adopted a representative democracy to effectively govern a vast and diverse nation.

Philosophical Perspectives on Democracy: Ancient Greek Views and Modern Interpretations

Classical Greek philosophy is the foundation of Western thought, with influential figures such as Socrates, Plato, and Aristotle shaping ideas about governance, ethics, and societal structure. Although their views on democracy vary, they offer valuable perspectives on the ancient Athenian model and its significance in today's political discussions.

Views of Greek Philosophers on Democracy

The ancient Greek philosophers had a skeptical and critical view of democracy, which was quite different from the modern ideals. Socrates, for example, had concerns about the dangers that democracy could bring. He worried that if the majority had unchecked power, it could lead to instability and injustice. Socrates famously argued that governance should be entrusted to individuals who possess wisdom and moral integrity, as they would make decisions in the best interest of the city-state.

Plato, who was a disciple of Socrates, took an even more critical stance. In his famous work "The Republic," Plato presented a society with a hierarchical structure governed by philosopher-kings. He questioned whether the masses were capable of governing wisely. Plato feared that democracy, with its emphasis on freedom and equality among citizens, could easily descend into anarchy or demagoguery, undermining the pursuit of justice and virtue.

Aristotle, on the other hand, was more accepting of democracy in principle but acknowledged its flaws. He classified democracy as a form of government where the majority holds power, often neglecting the interests of the minority. Aristotle also recognized the potential for mob rule and the inherent instability that comes with purely democratic systems.

Modern Views on Democracy

In the contemporary world, democracy is widely regarded as the most legitimate and just form of governance, characterized by electoral representation, rule of law, protection of minority rights, and civic participation. Unlike the ancient Greeks, modern democratic theory emphasizes inclusivity, deliberation, and accountability.

My personal view aligns with the modern understanding of democracy. I believe that democracy, when functioning effectively, ensures the collective voice of the people is heard through free and fair elections. It provides avenues for citizens to engage in policymaking, holds elected officials accountable through checks and balances, and safeguards fundamental rights and freedoms. Moreover, democracy fosters pluralism and diversity, allowing for the peaceful coexistence of differing opinions and interests within society.

Comparison and Reflection

The comparison between ancient Greek philosophical critiques and contemporary democratic practices shows a clear evolution and adaptation. While Socrates and Plato had concerns about direct democracy, modern democracies have made significant changes to address those concerns. They have introduced representative institutions and mechanisms to minimize the risks identified by these philosophers. Examples of these changes include judicial review, constitutional constraints on executive power, and independent judiciaries. These measures are crucial in ensuring the rule of law and protecting individual liberties.

In my own country, the United States, democracy operates with constitutional safeguards, separation of powers, and regular elections that uphold the principle of popular sovereignty. Citizens enjoy a wide range of civil liberties and participate in decision-making processes through representative democracy. However, we still face challenges such as political polarization, maintaining electoral integrity, and the influence of money in politics.

These challenges highlight the ongoing need for vigilance and active civic engagement.

Conclusion

Exploring the criticisms of democracy by Greek philosophers enhances our comprehension of its intricacies and obstacles. Their perspectives still stimulate contemplation and discussion on how to foster and maintain democratic principles in our present-day societies. By carefully analyzing both historical and contemporary viewpoints, we can gain a deeper understanding of the development of democratic theory and application, aiming for governance that upholds justice, equality, and the welfare of all.

Governmental Structures of Athens and Sparta: A Comparative Analysis

Ancient Greece had a fascinating history with various city-states, with Athens and Sparta standing out as powerful entities with contrasting forms of governance. This study delves into how these city-states allowed public involvement, selected officials, and compared and contrasted their governmental systems.

Acquisition of Political Participation Rights:

Athens: In ancient Athens, being a citizen meant actively participating in politics, although it was limited to a certain group of people. Only adult men who were free had the privilege to take part in the political affairs, making up around 10% of the total population. Their involvement mainly revolved around attending the Assembly (Ekklesia), where important matters like laws, war, and foreign policy were discussed and decided upon through voting. This system of direct democracy empowered citizens to express their views and bring about changes directly through their votes and public discussions (Rothchild, 2007).

Sparta: Sparta's political system was characterized by its militaristic and authoritarian nature, in stark contrast to Athens. Participation in politics was limited to male citizens who had undergone intense military training. Military strength and discipline were highly valued in

Sparta, with democratic processes taking a backseat. Leadership and decision-making were in the hands of the Gerousia, a council of elders, and the dual kingship, both of which were hereditary positions not subject to regular citizen voting (Brand, 2010).

Public Officeholders:

Athens: In ancient Athens, the process of choosing public officeholders was a mix of elections and random selection. The important roles of archons, who acted as top magistrates, and the members of the Council of 500 (Boule), who were in charge of suggesting and preparing laws, were not held by the same people for too long. This rotation system was put in place to avoid any individual or group from gaining too much power, and it encouraged a strong sense of civic responsibility and involvement (Brand, 2010).

Sparta: In ancient Sparta, the only public offices available were the dual kingship and the Gerousia, which consisted of older male citizens. The kings, who inherited their positions, had restricted powers and were counterbalanced by the Gerousia, which served as a decision-making group and held significant sway over state matters. The ephors, chosen every year through elections, acted as supervisors and had the ability to question the authority of the kings, providing a distinctive system of checks and balances in Spartan governance (Brand, 2010).

Rules Governing Selection of Officeholders:

Athens: In Athens, the process of choosing leaders was based on democratic ideals, where citizenship and qualifications were well-established. Those in office were supposed to advocate for the people and support democratic beliefs, guaranteeing responsibility through consistent evaluation and public hearings (Rothchild, 2007).

Sparta: Spartan officials were selected based on their age, military service achievements, and commitment to the traditional Spartan principles of discipline and loyalty to the state. The combination of having two kings and the Gerousia ensured that there was consistency and stability in the government, while the ephors were responsible for overseeing and regulating public affairs, ensuring that Spartan laws and customs were upheld (Brand, 2010).

Similarities and Differences in Governmental Structures:

Similarities: Athens and Sparta were both important city-states in ancient Greece, focusing on civic responsibility and allegiance to the state. While their political systems varied, they were designed to benefit the overall well-being of their communities. Additionally, they encouraged citizen involvement and had structures in place for making decisions and governing.

Differences:

- Athens encouraged its citizens to engage in direct democracy, which meant that everyone had a chance to participate in decision-making, although it was only open to adult males who were free.
- Sparta, on the other hand, placed importance on a diverse system of government that incorporated aspects of monarchy (dual kingship), oligarchy (Gerousia), and democracy (ephors). Their main focus was on military strength and maintaining control over the state.

Conclusion:

To sum it up, ancient Greece saw two different styles of governance in Athens and Sparta. Athens led the way with direct democracy, giving its people the power to actively participate in public affairs and make decisions.

On the other hand, Sparta opted for a centralized and militaristic system, placing importance on collective security and upholding traditional Spartan values. These distinct governmental approaches not only shaped the political landscapes of Athens and Sparta, but also left a lasting impact on political thinking and practices in the years to come.

Chapter 2

Social Structures and Cultural Practices in Ancient Greece

Contrasting Social Structures of Athens and Sparta

Slavery and Helotry:

Athens and Sparta differed markedly in their treatment of slaves and helots, respectively. In Athens, slavery was a fundamental institution, with slaves (often prisoners of war or debtors) performing various tasks ranging from domestic chores to skilled labor. They lacked political rights but could earn freedom through various means, such as purchasing it or being freed by their masters (Cartwright, 2018). Conversely, Sparta's economy heavily relied on helots, who were state-owned serfs tied to the land and obligated to provide agricultural produce to their Spartan masters. Helots lacked basic freedoms and were subjected to harsh treatment to maintain Spartan dominance (Culture in classical Sparta, n.d.).

Education Systems:

Education in Athens and Sparta reflected their respective societal values. Athenian education focused on intellectual and artistic development, particularly for boys who received formal schooling in subjects like rhetoric, mathematics, and philosophy. Girls, however, received limited education primarily focused on household management (Garland, 2020). In contrast, Spartan education emphasized physical fitness, discipline, and military training from an early age. Both boys and girls underwent rigorous physical education, aiming to produce competent warriors to uphold Sparta's militaristic society (Garland, 2020).

Position of Women:

The roles of women in Athens and Sparta diverged significantly. Athenian women had restricted rights and were primarily relegated to domestic duties. They had limited opportunities for education and participation in public life, their status largely defined by their male relatives (Cartwright, 2018). In contrast, Spartan women enjoyed more autonomy and were encouraged to participate in physical activities to ensure strong offspring for the state. They had greater freedom of movement and economic independence compared to their Athenian counterparts, albeit still under the overarching control of Spartan societal norms (Life in two city-states: Athens and Sparta, n.d.).

Athens and Sparta, two powerful Greek city-states, had distinct social structures when it came to slavery, education, and the status of women. These differences played a significant role in shaping their societies and impacting their contributions to Greek civilization.

The Role of Religion in Greek Society and Culture

In ancient Greek society, religion was a fundamental part of everyday life, shaping everything from politics and family dynamics to artistic endeavors and architectural designs. The Greeks followed a polytheistic faith, worshipping a variety of gods and goddesses, each with unique traits and areas of influence. This belief system not only directed their spiritual rituals but also had a profound impact on their cultural outputs, especially in the realms of art and architecture.

Greek Religion: Polytheistic Beliefs

Greek religion was primarily polytheistic, with the Greeks honoring a diverse range of gods believed to dwell in the heavens, on earth, and even in the underworld. The most notable deities, referred to as the Olympian gods, were thought to live on Mount Olympus and included figures like Zeus, the chief god; Athena, the goddess of wisdom and warfare; Apollo, the god of the sun and music; and Poseidon, the god of the ocean. Each god had unique traits, duties, and areas of influence, which were illustrated in the myths and tales central to Greek religious practices.

For instance, Zeus was celebrated as the ultimate ruler of the skies and weather, often shown with thunderbolts in hand. His might and authority were mirrored in the governance of Greek city-states, where rulers frequently claimed divine endorsement from Zeus to validate their leadership. Likewise, Athena, who sprang fully armed from Zeus's forehead, symbolized wisdom and battle, receiving particular reverence in Athens, where the Parthenon was built in her honor. The polytheistic aspect of Greek religion created a vibrant array of myths and ceremonies that differed from one city-state to another, yet all played a role in shaping a common cultural identity.

Influence of Religion on Greek Art

Religion had a significant impact on Greek art, shaping the way artists expressed their creativity. Greek creators often portrayed deities, divine figures, and mythological tales, highlighting the importance of these elements in their society. Religious motifs were prevalent across various artistic mediums, such as pottery, sculpture, and frescoes.

For example, Greek vase paintings frequently depicted stories from mythology, like the trials of Hercules or the journeys of Odysseus, who were thought to have the gods' favor. These narratives were not only captivating but also served to impart moral lessons and reinforce the cultural ideals tied to the divine.

Sculpture also played a vital role in showcasing the Greeks' religious fervor. Statues of gods and goddesses were commonly placed in temples and public areas. The statue of Zeus at Olympia, recognized as one of the Seven Wonders of the Ancient World, illustrates how deeply religion influenced some of the most remarkable artistic achievements. This grand statue represented not just the deity but also the divine connection in the everyday lives of the people.

Influence of Religion on Greek Architecture

Greek architecture, especially in the realm of temple building, was deeply shaped by the prevailing religious beliefs of the time. Temples served as earthly abodes for the gods, where people could perform rituals and make offerings. The architectural design aimed to embody the might of the deities and the devotion of the worshippers. The Parthenon in Athens stands out as a prime example of this religious architecture. Dedicated to Athena, the city's guardian goddess, the Parthenon was built to pay tribute to her and showcase Athens' wealth and influence. Its design, characterized by Doric columns and detailed sculptures, highlights the expertise of Greek architects and their ambition to create a space befitting the divine. Likewise, the Temple of Apollo at Delphi held great significance as a religious site. Home to the Oracle of Delphi, this temple was one of the most vital spiritual centers in the Greek world. Pilgrims traveled from far and wide to seek Apollo's guidance, illustrating the profound impact of religion on both social and political spheres.

Conclusion

To sum up, religion played a fundamental role in Greek society, influencing both spiritual beliefs and cultural manifestations in art and architecture. The polytheistic aspect of Greek religion offered a vibrant and varied lens through which to comprehend the universe and individual existence, a perspective that is beautifully showcased in the religious art and architecture that continues to inspire us today. From the majestic temples honoring the deities to the detailed sculptures and paintings illustrating their legends, Greek religion has profoundly shaped the cultural heritage of the ancient world.

The Enduring Legacy of Ancient Greece on Western Civilization

Introduction

Ancient Greece, often considered the birthplace of Western civilization, had a significant impact on modern society through its groundbreaking advancements in philosophy, democracy, art, and literature. This research investigates how Greek civilization continues to influence contemporary Western culture, demonstrating how the fundamental ideas and extraordinary achievements of ancient Greece still hold relevance in today's world. From the establishment of democratic rule in Athens to the enduring concepts of balance and harmony in Greek art and architecture, and from the philosophical musings of Socrates, Plato, and Aristotle to the timeless stories of Homer and the tragedies of Sophocles, the legacy of Ancient Greece is evident in every aspect of Western thought, governance, and artistic expression. This examination seeks to emphasize the deep and enduring influence of Classical Greece on shaping the intellectual, political, and cultural structures that characterize modern Western civilization.

Influence on Political Systems and Democracy

Ancient Greece, especially Athens, played a crucial role in shaping democratic governance, leaving a significant mark on political systems globally. The Athenian democratic system, which emerged in the 5th century BCE, was a major departure from earlier forms of government by actively involving its citizens in decision-making processes. Key institutions such as the ekklesia (assembly) and the dikasteria (courts) allowed ordinary citizens to debate, vote on legislation, and participate in judicial proceedings (Cartwright, 2018).

This direct form of democracy, supported by influential leaders like Pericles during Athens' Golden Age, promoted the ideals of equality under the law and civic responsibility. Citizens were encouraged to actively engage in public affairs, fostering a sense of collective ownership over governmental decisions. The Athenian model not only emphasized the empowerment of the populace but also laid the groundwork for principles fundamental to modern democratic societies, including the rule of law, individual rights, and governmental accountability (Cartwright, 2018).

The legacy of Athenian democracy extends beyond its historical context, serving as a benchmark for democratic governance in contemporary societies. Its emphasis on citizen participation and the protection of civil liberties continues to influence political thought and practice worldwide, illustrating the enduring impact of

Ancient Greece on the development of democratic institutions and values in the modern era.

Cultural and Artistic Legacy

Greek art and architecture showcase the principles of balance, harmony, and aesthetic perfection. The classical architectural orders of Doric, Ionic, and Corinthian are still evident in famous structures like the Parthenon and the United States Capitol. These styles remain influential in modern building design, representing the timeless beauty and enduring charm of Greek artistic values (Garland, 2020).

Additionally, Greek sculpture, known for its focus on naturalism and idealized figures, has had a significant impact on Western art. Masterpieces like the Discobolus and the Venus de Milo continue to motivate artists and sculptors, embodying the Greek belief in beauty and the human form as a reflection of divine proportions.

Philosophical Foundations

Greek philosophy, led by influential figures such as Socrates, Plato, and Aristotle, transformed the way we think and reason. Socrates' method of questioning assumptions and pursuing truth through dialogue set the stage for Western philosophical exploration. Plato's Republic delved into ideas of justice, governance, and the perfect society, leaving a lasting mark on political theory and ethical philosophy for generations to come (Cartwright, 2018).

Aristotle, in works like Nicomachean Ethics and Politics, established structured systems for understanding ethics, politics, and the natural world, molding Western perspectives on morality and leadership. Their timeless contributions to logic, metaphysics, and epistemology remain integral to scholarly discussions and ethical standards in contemporary society, underscoring the enduring influence of Greek philosophical thought (Garland, 2020).

Conclusion

The impact of Classical Greece on modern Western society and culture runs deep and wide. From the establishment of democratic governance to lasting principles of artistic expression and philosophical exploration, the civilization of Ancient Greece continues to influence the course of Western civilization. Its values of democracy, harmony, and intellectual rigor remain crucial in today's cultural standards and intellectual frameworks, highlighting the timeless significance of Greek accomplishments in shaping the world we inhabit today.

In essence, the lasting heritage of Ancient Greece stands as proof of the enduring strength of ideas and advancements that surpass time and location, enhancing our comprehension of democracy, aesthetics, and moral exploration in the contemporary age.

Chapter 3

The Greek Wars: From Preservation to Collapse

The Greco-Persian Wars: Preservation, Hegemony, and Cultural Legacy

The Greco-Persian Wars, occurring between 499 and 449 BCE, were a series of conflicts that greatly influenced the course of ancient Greek history. The battles, primarily involving the Greek city-states and the Persian Empire under the rule of Darius I and Xerxes I, left a lasting impact on Greece and the development of Western civilization (Boundless world history 1: Ancient civilizations – enlightenment - Version 35, 2022).

Preservation of Greek Autonomy and Cultural Identity

One of the most significant outcomes of the Greco-Persian Wars was the preservation of Greek autonomy and cultural identity. The Persian invasions, beginning with Darius I's expedition in 490 BCE and culminating in Xerxes I's massive invasion in 480 BCE, posed a direct threat to the sovereignty and independence of the Greek city-states. In response, Athens and Sparta, the two leading city-states, formed alliances and mobilized their forces to defend against the Persian incursions. Key battles such as the Battle of Marathon in 490 BCE, where the Athenians under Miltiades successfully repelled the Persian forces, demonstrated Greek military prowess and determination. Despite being outnumbered, the Greeks utilized superior tactics and strategy, including the famous phalanx formation, to achieve victory. This early success at Marathon galvanized Greek unity and provided a morale boost that would prove crucial in subsequent conflicts (Boundless world history 1: Ancient civilizations – enlightenment - Version 35, 2022).

Formation of the Delian League and Athenian Hegemony

Following the end of the war, the establishment of the Delian League in 478 BCE was a moment in Greek alliances and power dynamics. Initially created as a defensive pact against potential Persian threats, the Delian League gradually transformed into an Athenian empire under Athenian leadership. With its superior navy and strategic location, Athens took on a leading role within the league, effectively turning it into an Athenian hegemony. Led by figures like Themistocles and Pericles, Athens utilized the resources of the Delian League to boost its own economic prosperity and cultural influence. The wealth generated from member-states played a key role in the embellishment of Athens, including the construction of iconic structures like the Parthenon and other architectural wonders on the Acropolis. This era, known as the Golden Age of Athens, saw remarkable advancements in art, philosophy, and literature, showcasing the cultural peak achieved under Athenian dominance. (Cartwright, 2018; Boundless world history 1: Ancient civilizations – enlightenment - Version 35, 2022).

Cultural Confidence and Ideological Impact

The Greco-Persian Wars not only had military and political consequences but also boosted Greek cultural confidence and ideological superiority. The triumph over the Persian Empire reinforced Greek values of democracy, individual freedom, and civic responsibility. The rise of democracy in Athens, with more citizens participating in politics, showed a renewed dedication to democratic governance and civic involvement. Additionally, the wars fostered a sense of Greek exceptionalism and cultural pride. The victory of a coalition of Greek city-states over the vast Persian Empire highlighted the Greeks' belief in their unique cultural and intellectual contributions to the world. This cultural revival, sparked by the aftermath of the wars, set the stage for advancements in philosophy, historiography, and scientific exploration that characterised classical Greek civilization (Boundless world history 1: Ancient civilizations – enlightenment - Version 35, 2022).

Legacy and Historical Significance

The Greco-Persian Wars left a lasting impact on Greek history and Western civilization. By showcasing military bravery, forming strategic partnerships, and maintaining their cultural identity, the Greeks not only protected their land but also kickstarted a cultural revival that influenced Western philosophy and civilization. The influence of these wars goes beyond just military victories, as they also inspired enduring values like democracy, intellectual curiosity, and artistic creativity that still hold significance in today's world (Invicta, 2019; Cartwright, 2018).

Athens' Struggles During and After the Peloponnesian War: Strategic Failures and the Collapse of Democracy

Athens could not effectively handle the Peloponnesian War, do you agree? Why/why not? Support your answer with sources and evidence by providing details and examples.

I believe that Athens was unable to effectively manage the Peloponnesian War. This belief is backed by various reasons, such as strategic errors, internal conflicts, and external influences that all contributed to the collapse of Athenian democracy.

Athens made several strategic mistakes during the war. One notable blunder was the disastrous Athenian expedition to Sicily in 415 BCE. Thucydides, an ancient historian, extensively chronicled this failed campaign. According to him, the Athenian fleet, under the leadership of Alcibiades, suffered a crushing defeat, resulting in significant losses of both manpower and resources (Cartwright, 2018). This defeat not only diminished Athens' military strength but also dampened the spirits of its people and allies.

Secondly, the war exacerbated internal divisions within Athens. The prolonged conflict strained the city's political and social structures. During the war, Athens experienced a devastating plague (430-426 BCE) that killed a significant portion of its population, including the influential leader Pericles. According to the ancient historian Thucydides, the plague led to widespread lawlessness and weakened civic cohesion (Boundless World History, 2022). The loss of Pericles' leadership further destabilized the political environment, making it difficult for Athens to maintain a unified front.

The war had a significant economic impact as well. Athens faced financial strain from ongoing military expenses, with its trade-dependent economy suffering from the Spartan blockade and interruptions in grain shipments from the Black Sea. Additionally, the mismanagement of funds from the Delian League worsened the situation, as Athens diverted resources towards its own initiatives instead of collective defense efforts against Persia. This decision alienated allies, resulting in reduced support and uprisings against Athenian dominance (Boundless World History, 2022).

Is it correct to say that democracy in Athens was overthrown after the war?

Yes, it's true to say that democracy in Athens ended after the Peloponnesian War. The war's end brought about the emergence of an oligarchic regime known as the Thirty Tyrants, marking a significant departure from Athenian democratic principles.

The Thirty Tyrants were installed by Sparta after Athens' surrender in 404 BCE. This regime, led by Critias and supported by Spartan military presence, ruled through fear and repression. They executed many of their political opponents and confiscated property, leading to widespread disenfranchisement and terror among the populace (Scaliger, 2021). The establishment of the Thirty Tyrants effectively dismantled the democratic institutions that had been the hallmark of Athenian political life.

Moreover, the overthrow of Athenian democracy was not merely a result of external conquest but also stemmed from internal disillusionment and strife. The prolonged war had eroded public trust in the democratic process, as evidenced by the brief oligarchic coup of 411 BCE, when a group of wealthy Athenians attempted to establish an oligarchy to better manage the war effort. Although this coup was short-lived, it highlighted the vulnerability of Athenian democracy during times of crisis (Boundless World History, 2022).

The final blow to Athenian democracy came when Sparta, victorious in the war, sought to impose its own political model on Athens. The imposition of the Thirty Tyrants was part of a broader Spartan strategy to control and weaken its former adversary. The tyranny lasted only a year, but it caused significant damage to the democratic fabric of Athens. Eventually, democracy was restored in 403 BCE after a popular uprising led by Thrasybulus, but the experience left lasting scars on the Athenian psyche (Scaliger, 2021).

To sum up, the Peloponnesian War didn't just make Athens weaker in terms of military and economy, but it also set the stage for a temporary overthrow of its democracy. The challenges Athens faced internally and externally during and after the war highlight the city's struggle to handle the conflict and its aftermath, resulting in major political turmoil and the temporary absence of democratic rule.

Chapter 4

From Etruscan Roots to Roman Republic: An Exploration of Origins and Decline

Uncovering Roman-Etruscan Connections: Historical, Genetic, and Cultural Insights

It's important to look at both historical accounts and new genetic research to explore the possibility of the Romans being descended from the Etruscans. The Etruscans were a major civilization that existed before Rome, and their impact on Roman culture, government, and social customs is widely recorded.

According to historical accounts, the early days of Rome were greatly impacted by the Etruscans who lived nearby. The tale of Romulus and Remus, the legendary founders of Rome, is closely connected to the history of Rome's initial rulers, some of whom were Etruscan. This story suggests that the Romans not only took inspiration from the Etruscans but could also have Etruscan ancestry.

New genetic research has solidified the basis for this theory. A study, featured in Science Advances, examined the DNA of Etruscan-era remains and revealed that the Etruscans had genetic similarities with their Latin counterparts. This indicates a shared ancestry between the Etruscans and Romans. The study also indicated that the Etruscans were partially descended from European Stone Age farmers from around 6000 BCE, and later intermingled with migrants from the modern-day Russian and Ukrainian steppes (Curry, 2021).

Additionally, there is strong evidence from both cultural and archaeological sources indicating a notable Etruscan impact on the early Roman civilization. The Etruscans were recognized for their sophisticated engineering, religious customs, and societal systems, a number of which were embraced by the Romans. For instance, the Roman tradition of divination and the structure of their military can be linked back to Etruscan origins (Boundless, 2022).

The Etruscans had a significant influence on Roman architecture and urban planning. They are credited with building Rome's impressive sewer system, using their engineering expertise. Furthermore, the design of Roman cities, including their forums and public areas, reflects the urban planning of the Etruscans (DailyHistory.org, n.d.).

Lastly, the crossroads of historical stories, genetic proof, and cultural impacts provides compelling evidence that the Romans could have originated from the Etruscans. This lineage is evident that not just in common genetic characteristics but also in the cultural and societal advancements that the Etruscans brought to ancient Roman society.

The Fall of the Roman Republic: Analyzing Causes, Consequences, and Lessons for Modern Governance

The Roman Republic is often cited as a key example of early democratic governance, but its eventual downfall serves as a warning about the fragility of institutions and the difficulties of maintaining republican principles in the long run. By examining the reasons behind its collapse, historians have uncovered the intricate factors that eroded its political foundation and ultimately brought about its end.

Factors Contributing to the Fall of the Roman Republic

Several factors contributed to the decline of the Roman Republic, each playing a significant role in weakening its political structure and social cohesion:

1. **Political Corruption and Ambition**: The decline of the Republic was significantly influenced by the unbridled ambition of political elites. As Rome expanded its territory, the competition for power and wealth intensified among the ruling class. Political offices became opportunities for personal enrichment rather than serving the common good (Bobertz, 2022).
2. **Military Instability and Command Loyalty**: The growing dependence on military leaders like Sulla and Caesar, who led loyal legions and

exploited them for their own political advantage, disrupted the traditional power balance within the Republic. This militarization of politics weakened the Senate's authority and fueled civil unrest (Shiffer, 2021).

3. **Social and Economic Inequality**: The expansion of Rome led to an increase in wealth, however, it also opened economic inequalities. Small farmers and urban plebeians experienced difficulties, as landowners expanded their estates using slave labor and exploitation (Brown, 2016).

4. **Failure of Republican Institutions**: The traditional republican institutions, originally intended for a city-state, faced difficulties in adjusting to the demands of governing a vast empire. The Senate, which used to be a forum for discussion and decision-making, found itself becoming less efficient and incapable of tackling the expanding social and economic problems that plagued Rome (Democracy in troubled times, 2021).

Identifying the Most Significant Factor

The decline of the Republic can be attributed to a variety of factors, but the most significant was political corruption and ambition. This issue affected all aspects of Roman society and government, causing a loss of faith in the institutions and resulting in a cycle of turmoil and discord.

Mitigating the Damage

Reducing the damage caused by political corruption could have potentially preserved the Roman Republic or at least prolonged its stability:

1. **Reform of Electoral Practices**: Implementing stricter regulations on campaign financing, implement term limits for political offices, and creating mechanisms for transparency could have reduced the influence of wealthy elites and promoted a more merit-based system (Brown, 2016).
2. **Strengthening Civic Virtue**: Focusing on civic education and moral values within the education system may have helped instill a sense of duty and responsibility in political leaders, encouraging integrity and accountability in public service (Democracy in troubled times, 2021).

3. **Balancing Power Dynamics**: Implementing checks and balances in the political system, like those found in contemporary democracies, could have stopped power from being consolidated by certain individuals and/or military leaders (Shiffer, 2021).

4. **Addressing Socioeconomic Inequality**: Implement land reforms, supporting small farmers, and creating economic opportunities for the urban poor could have helped alleviate social unrest and decreased the attractiveness of populist leaders who took advantage of economic grievances (Bobertz, 2022).

Conclusion

In conclusion, although the Roman Republic is often seen as an admirable example of democratic governance, its collapse highlights the significance of political corruption and unchecked duties to uphold political stability. By acknowledging historical errors and putting measures into place to foster ethical leadership and equality, communities can fortify their democratic systems and guarantee their endurance amidst changing circumstances.

Unraveling the Roman-Etruscan Connection: Historical, Archaeological, and Genetic Insights

The inquiry into whether the Romans originated from the Etruscans involves a deep dive into history, combining archaeological findings, cultural parallels, and ancient writings to uncover the connection between these two ancient civilizations. This conversation seeks to thoroughly examine these aspects, offering a thorough investigation of the possible genetic and cultural links between the Etruscans and Romans.

The Etruscans, a civilization that flourished in central Italy before Rome's dominance, had a significant impact on early Roman culture. Excavations have revealed a plethora of artifacts demonstrating the close relationship between the Etruscans and Romans. For instance, the city of Rome itself bears traces of Etruscan influence in its urban planning, religious practices, and artistic styles (Shiffer, 2021). The architectural techniques brought by the Etruscans, including arches and sewer systems, played a crucial role in shaping the infrastructure and cityscape of Rome.

Archaeological digs in places such as Veii, Cerveteri, and Tarquinia have uncovered striking parallels in how the Etruscans and early Romans handled burials, crafted pottery, and used artistic themes (Bobertz, 2022). The results indicate a long-lasting cultural connection and exchange between the two societies instead of an abrupt separation or interruption.

Genetic research hasn't definitively proven a direct link between the Etruscans and the Romans, but it has revealed the genetic variety present in ancient Rome. Studies show a mix of Mediterranean and Central European genetic traits in the Roman population, showcasing the city's role as a melting pot for different cultures and peoples(Brown, 2016). Rome's genetic diversity highlights its status as a diverse hub where different ethnicities mixed and influenced the city's genetic composition.

Ancient Roman historians like Livy and Dionysius of Halicarnassus offer valuable information about the connection between the Etruscans and Romans. They describe cultural exchanges, political partnerships, and occasional disagreements, showing a complex and diverse relationship that lasted for centuries (Shiffer, 2021).

Ancient Roman historians like Livy and Dionysius of Halicarnassus offer valuable information about the connection between the Etruscans and Romans. They describe cultural exchanges, political partnerships, and occasional disagreements, showing a complex and diverse relationship that lasted for centuries.

Chapter 5

Comparative Strategies and Outcomes: Sparta vs. Rome, Cleopatra's Diplomatic Dilemmas, and the Rome-Macedon Rivalry

Comparative Analysis of Sparta and Rome: Strategies, Goals, and Conquests

Sparta and Rome were both formidable city-states aiming for supremacy in their own territories, yet their approaches and goals were quite distinct.

Similarities

1. Desire for Dominance: Sparta and Rome both strived to assert their power in their own territories. Sparta focused on dominating the Greek city-states and establishing its supremacy, whereas Rome aimed to bring together the Italian Peninsula and extend its reach further.
2. Military Aggression: Both city-states utilized military force in their strategies. Sparta relied on its powerful army to attack Athens and its supporters, whereas Rome conducted multiple military operations to conquer the city-states in Italy and the Carthaginian empire.

Differences

1. Strategic Goals: Sparta's primary goal in the Peloponnesian War was to break Athenian dominance and maintain its own hegemony over the Peloponnesian League. The war was largely defensive and aimed at preserving the existing

balance of power (UNRV Roman History, n.d.). In contrast, Rome's expansion was more aggressive and aimed at territorial and political dominance, leading to the consolidation of the Italian Peninsula and the defeat of Carthage (Coco, 2019).
2. Scope of Conquest: Sparta only conquered Greece, with a main focus on Athens and its allies. In contrast, Rome went on to conquer territories far beyond Italy, stretching across the Mediterranean into Asia and Africa (Ancient Rome Live, 2020; Wasson, 2016).
3. Political and Economic Factors: Sparta's motivations were influenced by a desire to maintain its oligarchic system and suppress democratic Athens (UNRV Roman History, n.d.). Rome's motivations included economic benefits from controlling trade routes and resources in the conquered regions (Immacolata, 2015).

Conclusion

To sum up, Sparta and Rome both pursued military campaigns to gain power, but their goals and tactics were influenced by different strategic objectives and political environments. Sparta aimed for dominance within

Greece, while Rome had larger ambitions, aiming for control over the wider Mediterranean region and beyond.

Cleopatra VII and the Roman Power Struggle: Strategies for Preserving Egyptian Independence

Introduction

Cleopatra VII, the last reigning leader of the Ptolemaic Kingdom of Egypt, encountered a turbulent era filled with significant political and military obstacles. Wasson (2016) noted that Cleopatra found herself "unfortunately caught in the middle of a power struggle." This study delves into the power struggle mentioned by Wasson and proposes potential tactics Cleopatra could have used to prevent the Roman takeover of Egypt.

The Power Struggle:

Wasson (2016) highlights a power struggle centered on Cleopatra's role in Roman political affairs. Cleopatra faced internal conflicts in Egypt, particularly with her brother Ptolemy XIII, which resulted in a civil war and destabilized the region. While her alliance with Julius Caesar initially benefited her, it also made her vulnerable to opposition from figures like Octavian (later Emperor Augustus).

Cleopatra's role in Roman politics had both positive and negative consequences. Her partnerships with Julius Caesar and later Mark Antony were calculated decisions to protect her authority and Egypt's interests. However, these alliances also made her a target for Octavian, who viewed her as a rival and obstacle to his own goals. The complex and ever-changing political environment in Rome ultimately contributed to Cleopatra's downfall (Immacolata, 2015).

Strategies to Avoid Roman Conquest:

Cleopatra had various options to prevent the Roman conquest.

1. **Strengthening Internal Unity:** It was crucial for Cleopatra to handle internal disagreements and strengthen her authority in Egypt. By settling disputes with Ptolemy XIII and showing a unified stance, she could have bolstered Egypt's defenses and engaged in more successful negotiations with Rome.
2. **Neutral Diplomatic Engagement:** Cleopatra could have chosen to pursue a diplomatic strategy that maintained Egypt's independence by establishing a treaty or alliance with Rome, rather than forming strong alliances with Julius Caesar and Mark Antony. This approach could have helped prevent direct conflict and acknowledged Roman influence while still preserving Egypt's autonomy.
3. **Enhancing Economic and Military Strength:** By enhancing Egypt's military and economic assets,

Cleopatra could have bolstered the country's defense against Roman expansion. Strengthening military prowess and safeguarding trade routes might have transformed Egypt into a stronger adversary and a key ally for Rome, possibly preventing Roman hostility.

4. **Strategic Marriages:** Cleopatra may have been able to use strategic marriages with influential Roman figures to safeguard Egypt's position. By forming alliances through marriage, she could have potentially navigated the Roman political landscape more effectively and protected Egypt's interests.

Conclusion

Cleopatra VII's downfall was impacted by internal conflicts and the intricate power dynamics within Rome. To prevent the Roman conquest, Cleopatra might have concentrated on internal unity, pursued neutral diplomacy, strengthened Egypt's economic and military power, and arranged strategic marriages. These actions could have assisted her in navigating the power struggles of the era and maintaining Egypt's independence.

100

The Rome-Macedon Rivalry: Causes, Key Events, and Consequences

Introduction

The rivalry between Rome and Macedon is a pivotal part of Roman expansion history. The four Macedonian Wars, which took place from 214 BCE to 148 BCE, played a key role in shaping the power balance in the ancient Mediterranean region. This study aims to delve into the reasons behind the conflict, pinpoint the most impactful event in the Rome-Macedonian wars, and examine the aftermath of Macedonia's loss to Rome.

Causes of the Conflict:

1. **Expansionist Ambitions:** Rome's desire to expand was a major factor in causing the conflict. As Rome strengthened its control in the Italian Peninsula, it aimed to spread its influence into the Greek world. Macedon, led by Philip V and later his son Perseus, was a major force in the eastern Mediterranean and a natural competitor to Roman expansion (UNRV Roman History, n.d.).
2. **Alliances and Rivalries:** The changing partnerships within the Greek world played a role in the conflict as well. Macedon's alliances with different Greek city-states and its resistance to Rome's influence in the area led to tensions. For example, the collaboration between Macedon and

Hannibal in the Second Macedonian War was viewed as a clear challenge to Rome (Wasson, 2016).

3. **Economic and Strategic Interests:** Rome sought to control important trade routes and key territories in the eastern Mediterranean in order to gain economic advantages and strategic benefits, leading to rivalry with Macedon (Coco, 2019).

Most Significant Event of the Rome-Macedonian Conflict:

The Battle of Pydna in 168 BCE was the key event in the Rome-Macedonian conflict. This important battle brought an end to the Third Macedonian War and resulted in the downfall of King Perseus of Macedon. The victory at Pydna held great significance for a number of reasons.

1. **Decisive Victory:** The Battle of Pydna marked a significant triumph for the Romans, putting an end to Macedonian opposition. It highlighted Rome's military strength and reinforced its control over the area. (UNRV Roman History, n.d.).

2. **Political and Strategic Implications:** After Perseus was defeated, the Macedonian Kingdom split into four client republics, which marked the end of Macedonian influence in Greece. As a result,

Rome was able to strengthen its hold over the eastern Mediterranean. (Coco, 2019).

Consequences of Macedonia's Defeat by Rome:

1. **Political Changes:** After Macedonia's loss, the kingdom was split into four republics, all eventually taken over by Rome. This breakup weakened Macedonian power and brought the region under Roman authority (Wasson, 2016).
2. **Roman Expansion:** The fall of Macedon was a crucial moment in Rome's push into the eastern Mediterranean. It set the stage for Rome to assert control over Greece and beyond, ultimately laying the foundation for the mighty Roman Empire (Coco, 2019).
3. **Cultural and Economic Integration:** The fall of Macedon made it easier for Greek culture and economic systems to become part of the Roman Empire. This merging helped to expand Roman influence and blend Greek and Roman traditions together (UNRV Roman History, n.d.).

Conclusion

The rivalry between Rome and Macedon was fueled by a mix of territorial ambitions, changing allegiances, and strategic goals. The Battle of Pydna is highlighted as a pivotal moment because of its profound influence on the war's result and the subsequent reorganization of the area's politics. The aftermath of Macedon's loss reshaped the Mediterranean's political scene, paving the way for Rome's growth and dominance. Exploring these interactions provides important perspectives on Rome's ascent as a major player in ancient times.

Chapter 6

Education, Slavery, and Gender Roles in Ancient Greek and Roman Societies

Evolution of Educational Practices: Comparing Ancient Roman Gender-Specific Education with Modern Reforms

During ancient times in Rome, the education for boys and girls was quite distinct. Boys typically received instruction in areas like politics, public speaking, and military tactics, which equipped them for involvement in public and political affairs. On the other hand, girls' education centered around domestic abilities, like running a household and upholding societal standards (Britannica, n.d.). This gender-specific method of education mirrored the wider societal norms and preferences.

When I look at the education system in my country, I can see both similarities and differences. In the past, girls had limited educational opportunities and were mainly taught traditional domestic roles, similar to ancient Roman practices. However, today's educational systems have changed to provide more equal opportunities for all genders, with a focus on subjects like STEM, humanities, and social sciences, regardless of gender (Aldrete, 2020).

If I were in charge of revamping the education system. I would suggest various changes to promote fairness and efficiency. To start, I would push for a curriculum that focuses on critical thinking and problem solving abilities for all students--- regardless of gender and going beyond traditional subject boundaries. This strategy would help students develop adaptable skills to thrive in a rapidly evolving world. Moreover, I would make sure that educational materials are inclusive and reflect a variety of perspectives, encouraging a more holistic view of the world. Lastly, I would introduce mentorship initiatives to inspire students to explore interests and careers that have been traditionally associated with the opposite gender, aiming to provide equal opportunities and break stereotypes.

Comparative Analysis of Slavery and Women's Roles in Ancient Greece and Rome

Introduction

Both Greek and Roman societies placed great importance on slavery and the role of women. However, they had unique approaches in how they viewed and treated slaves and women. This study delves into the lives of slaves in Greece and Rome, while also exploring the level of societal involvement of Roman women compared to Greek women. Through examples and evidence, we aim to provide a thorough analysis of these differences.

Life of Greek vs. Roman Slaves

Living Conditions

Greek and Roman slaves made important contributions to their societies, but their living situations were quite different. In Athens, Greek slaves had chances to work in skilled jobs and potentially gain their freedom. They served as household workers, artisans, or in government positions, offering a level of stability. On the other hand, Roman slaves endured tougher circumstances, often forced into exhausting work in mines or on vast latifundia estates. The severe treatment of Roman slaves, who faced harsh punishments, stands in sharp contrast to the relatively milder conditions that some Greek slaves enjoyed.

Legal Status and Rights

In ancient Greece, slaves had some legal rights and could take part in specific religious events, giving them a bit of social interaction outside of their servitude. On the other hand, Roman slaves were seen as property with very few legal protections, highlighting their status as possessions rather than individuals with rights.

Social Mobility and Manumission

Greek and Roman slaves experienced varying levels of social mobility and chances of manumission. Greek slaves, especially those with skills, had higher likelihood of being freed and could potentially blend into society, although they still encountered obstacles. On the other hand, Roman slaves had fewer chances of gaining freedom, and even if they were liberated, they usually stayed in a lower social class. The Roman patron-client system guaranteed that freed slaves would still serve their previous owners, restricting their upward mobility.

Conclusion on Slavery

Greek slaves typically had slightly better living conditions and more chances for upward mobility than Roman slaves. The severe mistreatment and strict laws imposed on Roman slaves highlight the stark contrasts between the two cultures.

Activity of Roman vs. Greek Women

Legal Rights and Status

Roman women had more rights and status compared to Greek women. They could own property, run businesses, and have some influence in public life. In contrast, women in Athens were mostly restricted to the household and had very limited public presence and legal rights. Spartan women had more freedom than Athenian women, but still did not have the same level of autonomy as Roman women.

Social and Public Roles

Roman women had a more prominent presence in social and public spheres than Greek women. Elite Roman women had the ability to impact politics through their family ties and take part in various social gatherings. They were actively engaged in religious practices and had the opportunity to support public projects and activities. On the other hand, Greek women, particularly in Athens, were typically required to stay out of the public eye, focusing mainly on running the household.

Examples of Prominent Women

Well-known Roman women like Livia Drusilla and Cornelia Africana showcase the significant impact women could have in society. Livia, Emperor Augustus's wife, wielded political power and played a key role in her son Tiberius's rise to power. Cornelia, mother of the Gracchi brothers, was admired for her wisdom and virtue, shaping her sons' political paths. On the other hand, Greek women in public roles, such as Aspasia of Miletus, were uncommon and frequently met with societal judgment.

Conclusion on Women's Activity

Roman women played a more significant role in society compared to Greek women, thanks to their greater legal rights, participation in public and religious affairs, and the presence of influential female figures.

Overall Conclusion

Both Greek and Roman societies heavily relied on slavery and placed significant restrictions on women. However, Roman slaves faced harsher conditions and had fewer chances for social mobility. On the other hand, Roman women had more rights and played more active roles in society compared to their Greek counterparts.

These differences emphasize the diverse and intricate nature of ancient civilizations in terms of slavery and the status of women.

Chapter 7
Assimilation and Evolution: The Influence of Greek Religion and Philosophy on Roman Culture

From Greek Gods to Roman Rituals: The Evolution and Adaptation of Religious Practices

Introduction

The impact of Greek religion on Roman religious customs has been extensively recorded, as numerous Greek deities were adapted into Roman mythology. This study aims to delve into the assimilation of five Greek gods into Roman worship, examine whether Roman religious practices were simply copied from the Greeks or evolved distinct traits, and shed light on an intriguing Roman religious ceremony.

Greek Gods in Roman Religion

Zeus was a prominent figure in Greek mythology, later becoming Jupiter in Roman religion, both representing the king of gods with authority and power. Hera, also known as Juno in Roman mythology, symbolized marriage and family. Ares, the Greek god of war, was transformed into Mars in Rome, embodying martial valor. Aphrodite, the goddess of love, was named Venus in Rome, symbolizing beauty and love. Lastly, Hermes, the messenger god, became Mercury, associated with commerce and communication.

Comparison and Evolution of Roman Religion

Roman religion took a lot of inspiration from Greek mythology, but it also adapted to reflect Roman values and social customs. For instance, the Romans focused on the practical and civic dimensions of religion, which resulted in a more organized and government-regulated system of worship (Grant, 2022). A unique aspect of Roman religion was the imperial cult, where emperors were worshipped as gods, distinguishing it from Greek traditions.

Fascinating Roman Religious Ritual or Practice

One intriguing Roman tradition is the Lupercalia, an ancient celebration that took place on February 15. During this festival, priests called Luperci would dash through the streets, playfully hitting people with thongs crafted from the hides of sacrificed goats. This ritual was thought to cleanse the city and enhance fertility (Grant, 2022). The blend of purification and fertility practices made this a distinctive and captivating element of Roman religious customs.

Conclusion

The incorporation of Greek deities into Roman spirituality and the development of these customs showcase the ever-changing aspect of religious faiths. Exploring these transformations offers a glimpse into the Roman perspective on their surroundings and their role in it.

Cultural Crossroads: The Impact of Greek Religion on Roman Art, Architecture, and Philosophy

Introduction

The Roman civilization, celebrated for its advancements in art, architecture, and philosophy, has been deeply shaped by Greek culture. This paper examines the impact of local religious beliefs on a nation's artistic and architectural expressions, while also investigating the connections between Roman and Greek philosophical thought. Additionally, it emphasizes the three primary schools of Roman philosophy and considers the personal resonance of these philosophical concepts.

Part A: Influence of Regional Religious Beliefs on Art and Architecture

The influence of regional religious beliefs has consistently been significant in molding a country's art and architecture. In ancient Rome, these beliefs were closely linked to everyday life, and this connection was evident in their artistic creations. Roman temples, sculptures, and paintings transcended mere aesthetics; they embodied symbols of religious faith and governmental authority (Cartwright, 2017). The impressive design of landmarks such as the Pantheon and the intricate adornments found in temples underscore the vital role religion played in Roman culture.

A great example is the Pantheon, which was initially constructed as a temple dedicated to all the Roman deities. It highlights the remarkable architectural advancements of the Romans, particularly with its impressive dome and oculus. The design represents the sky and the ever-present nature of the gods, illustrating how architecture intertwined with religious beliefs (Cartwright, 2018). In a similar vein, the reliefs and frescoes adorning Roman temples and public structures frequently illustrated mythological scenes, religious ceremonies, and deities, thereby reinforcing the cultural values and spiritual practices of that era.

In today's world, regional religious beliefs still play a significant role in shaping architecture and art. For example, in numerous Islamic nations, mosques are adorned with elaborate geometric designs and calligraphy, as Islamic art forbids the representation of human figures. Architectural features like minarets and domes are crafted to elevate the spiritual experience and symbolize the divine presence (Amber, n.d.). Likewise, in mainly Christian countries, churches frequently showcase stained glass windows that illustrate biblical stories, thereby reinforcing religious teachings and values.

It's clear that there is a strong link between religion and art in ancient as well as contemporary societies. Artists and architects often use religious beliefs as inspiration to produce pieces that are not only visually appealing but also hold spiritual significance. These artistic creations play a role in shaping the cultural and social fabric of the community.

Part B: Relationship Between Roman and Greek Philosophy

Roman philosophy was significantly shaped by Greek philosophy, especially following Rome's takeover of Greece. The Romans had a reputation for their pragmatic mindset, which they wove into their philosophical discussions. Greek philosophy, focusing on reason, ethics, and the cosmos, offered a robust base for Roman intellectuals (Juez, 2020). Nevertheless, Roman philosophers tailored these concepts to fit their own cultural environment, highlighting the importance of practicality and the relevance of philosophy in everyday life.

The three primary branches of Roman philosophy include Stoicism, Epicureanism, and Neoplatonism. Stoicism, established by Zeno of Citium, highlighted the importance of reason, self-discipline, and moral integrity as essential for a fulfilling life. It encouraged individuals to embrace the natural order of the universe and to remain unaffected by external circumstances (TED-Ed, 2017). Epicureanism, introduced by Epicurus, centered on seeking pleasure and steering clear of pain as life's main objectives. Nevertheless, it promoted the idea of enjoying simple pleasures and engaging in intellectual activities rather than indulging in excessive physical pleasures (Juez, 2020). Neoplatonism, which drew from Plato's teachings, focused on the concept of a singular, ultimate reality known as "the One." It proposed that the physical world mirrors a higher spiritual realm, with the soul's purpose being to reunite with this ultimate source (Renewing Greek Philosophy at Rome, n.d.).

Out of all these philosophies, Stoicism is the one that I find most appealing. Its focus on logic and emotional strength provides useful advice for dealing with life's obstacles. The concept of concentrating on what we can control and embracing what we cannot aligns well with today's efforts towards mental health. For instance, in our everyday lives, Stoicism can be implemented through mindfulness, changing negative perspectives, and staying composed during tough times. These techniques aid in developing inner tranquility and a clear direction, irrespective of external factors.

Conclusion

Roman culture was greatly impacted by Greek culture, but it also developed its own unique values and societal requirements. The incorporation of religious beliefs into art and the transformation of Greek philosophical concepts demonstrate the dynamic relationship between tradition and creativity. Studying these elements of Roman civilization offers important perspectives on how ancient societies have influenced the world today.

Chapter 8
The Modern Advantage: Advancements in Art, Architecture, and Philosophy Compared to Ancient Times

The Modern Age: Advancements in Art, Politics, Technology, and Law Compared to Ancient Times

140

If I had the chance to talk about why the modern age could be seen as a more favorable time to live than ancient times, I would point out numerous important developments that have improved both human life and society.

To begin with, the evolution of art and architecture in modern times presents a strong case. Although ancient Greek and Roman art established the groundwork for classical beauty, today's art and architecture have broadened and enriched these traditions like never before. For example, recent breakthroughs in construction materials and methods, including sustainable design and cutting-edge engineering, have transformed how we build and interact with our environments (Tschierse, 2022). This advancement marks a remarkable shift from the classical design principles.

Additionally, the development of political ideas highlights the significant progress we've made since the days of ancient governance. While ancient Greek democracy was a pioneering concept, it was restricted to a narrow group of individuals, often leaving out women and slaves (Cartledge, 2016). Today's democratic systems aim for enhanced inclusivity and representation, embodying a wider and fairer interpretation of democratic principles (Jones, 2022). This transformation illustrates a remarkable advancement in our political frameworks and practices.

Moreover, the advancements in culture and technology in today's world have significantly changed our daily lives. The philosophical and literary achievements of ancient Greece laid the groundwork for future intellectual progress (Gokhale, 2021). In contrast, our current global culture thrives on these early contributions, enhanced by cutting-edge technology that allows for immediate communication, vast access to information, and cultural interactions like never before (Owlcation, 2022). The degree of connectivity and knowledge we enjoy today would have been beyond comprehension in ancient times.

Finally, the impact of Greco-Roman concepts on today's legal and governmental structures showcases the advancements achieved over thousands of years. The foundations of ancient Roman law and governance have played a significant role in forming modern legal systems, which have evolved and broadened these ideas to tackle current challenges and promote a more inclusive sense of justice (Appletone, 2022).

To sum up, although the Greeks and Romans played a crucial role in shaping civilization, the developments in art, architecture, political ideas, technology, and legal frameworks highlight why our current era provides a more enriched and secure way of living. The advancements we've made not only honor their legacy but also exceed their accomplishments in numerous fields.

Enduring Legacies: The Influence of Greco-Roman Culture on Modern Art, Technology, and Philosophy

The ancient civilizations of Greece and Rome have profoundly influenced the world we live in today. Even after thousands of years since their decline, their contributions in culture, philosophy, and technology remain integral to our modern existence. This paper delves into how various aspects of Greco-Roman culture, such as art, architecture, and technological advancements, form the bedrock of contemporary society.

Art and Architecture

The impact of Greco-Roman civilization is prominently seen in today's art and architecture. Ancient Greek art, celebrated for its focus on proportion, balance, and idealized forms, has established a standard for classical beauty that remains relevant. Iconic Greek sculptures, like the Venus de Milo and the Parthenon sculptures, have significantly shaped Western artistic traditions (Tschierse, 2022). These classical principles continue to resonate in modern art, where symmetry and proportion are still valued, and classical themes and techniques are preserved in contemporary sculpture and painting.

Roman architecture has also played a crucial role in shaping modern building practices through its engineering innovations. The Romans pioneered the use of concrete, arches, and vaulted ceilings, allowing for the creation of monumental structures such as the Colosseum and the Pantheon (Tschierse, 2022). These architectural breakthroughs are evident in today's buildings, which often employ similar methods to achieve both structural strength and visual appeal. For example, the incorporation of arches and domes in modern public structures and monuments can be traced back to Roman architectural advancements (Appletone, 2022).

Technology

The technological contributions of Greco-Roman civilization, while often underestimated, have played a crucial role in shaping modern innovations. The Romans were trailblazers in creating infrastructure, particularly with their aqueducts, which transformed water supply systems (Owlcation, 2022). Their exceptional engineering skills in constructing roads and bridges enhanced communication and trade throughout their empire, establishing the groundwork for contemporary transportation systems. The engineering principles developed by the Romans are still relevant today in the design and building of modern infrastructure, highlighting the enduring influence of their technological advancements (Tschierse, 2022).

Moreover, the Greeks made significant strides in mathematics and science that have greatly influenced technological progress. Renowned Greek thinkers like Archimedes and Euclid laid the groundwork for geometry and mechanics, which remain essential to current scientific and engineering methodologies (Gokhale, 2021). Their contributions to mathematics and physics have been vital in advancing technology, from fundamental engineering concepts to intricate computer algorithms.

Philosophy and Literature

The philosophical legacies of ancient Greece have significantly shaped contemporary thought. Thinkers like Socrates, Plato, and Aristotle laid down essential principles for ethical reasoning, political theory, and the study of knowledge, which still resonate in today's philosophical and political discussions (Jones, 2022). Their insights into democracy, morality, and the essence of knowledge are fundamental to modern philosophy and political theory, influencing our current understanding and interaction with these ideas.

In the realm of literature, the contributions of Greek and Roman writers have left a profound mark on Western literary traditions. Epic poetry from Greece, such as Homer's Iliad and Odyssey, along with Roman works like Virgil's Aeneid, have established narrative frameworks and themes that remain central to contemporary storytelling (Gokhale, 2021). These literary masterpieces not only shape various forms and genres but also continue to motivate writers and artists, showcasing the lasting significance of Greco-Roman literary heritage.

Conclusion

The remarkable cultural, artistic, and technological advancements of ancient Greece and Rome have created a strong base for today's society. Their influence on art and architecture is still evident in modern design, and their technological breakthroughs and philosophical concepts are essential to current practices and ideas. The lasting legacy of Greco-Roman civilization emphasizes their significant role in shaping Western culture and showcases how their contributions continue to be relevant in our world today.

Conclusion

The lasting impact of ancient Greece and Rome on today's civilization highlights the significant role these classical cultures have played in shaping our modern society. This chapter has examined how the achievements of these ancient peoples in areas like art, architecture, technology, philosophy, and literature have created a strong foundation for the world we live in now. Their legacies continue to resonate, enrich, and inspire many facets of our lives, from the buildings we construct to the ideas we explore.

In the realms of art and architecture, the standards set by Greek and Roman pioneers have established lasting benchmarks for beauty and design. The Greek focus on proportion and balance, along with Roman innovations like concrete and arches, have left a mark on countless generations of artists and architects. Today's structures and artistic endeavors frequently reference these classical traditions, showcasing the enduring significance of Greco-Roman aesthetics and engineering.

The advancements in technology can be greatly attributed to the creativity of the Greeks and Romans. The Romans made significant strides in infrastructure, creating aqueducts, roads, and bridges that serve as the foundation for today's engineering and transportation systems. Meanwhile, the Greeks made essential contributions to mathematics and science, which have been crucial in the evolution of technological methods and innovations. The pioneering efforts of Greek mathematicians and Roman engineers underscore the lasting influence of their technological breakthroughs on modern practices.

The philosophical and literary contributions from the Greco-Roman period have profoundly shaped our intellectual and cultural heritage. The ethical and political ideas put forth by Greek thinkers like Socrates, Plato, and Aristotle continue to resonate in today's philosophical discussions. Likewise, the narrative styles and themes introduced by ancient Greek and Roman authors remain vital to modern literature and storytelling, showcasing the lasting importance of their literary contributions.

To sum up, the influence of ancient Greece and Rome goes beyond mere historical interest; it represents a vibrant heritage that actively shapes our contemporary world. Their remarkable contributions have laid a profound cultural and intellectual groundwork for today's society. By recognizing the extensive impact of Greco-Roman traditions, we gain insight into how ancient concepts and innovations have been reinterpreted and evolved, maintaining their importance in our current lives. Exploring these classical civilizations uncovers a continuous conversation between history and modernity, showcasing how the accomplishments of the past still motivate and affect our lives today.

Bibliography

Ancient Rome Live. (2020, October 30). Rome's conquest of Italy: 509-272 BCE. YouTube. Retrieved from https://www.youtube.com/watch?v=example

Aldrete, G. S. (2020, December 29). The role of women in Ancient Rome–piecing together a historical picture. WondriumDaily. Retrieved from https://my.uopeople.edu/pluginfile.php/1864711/mod_book/chapter/515321/The%20role%20of%20women%20in%20Ancient%20Rome%E2%80%94piecing%20together%20a%20historical%20picture..pdf?time=1703319072634

Appletone, S. (2022, October 12). Traces of Ancient Rome in the Modern World. National Geographic Society. Retrieved from https://education.nationalgeographic.org/resource/traces-ancient-rome-modern-world/

Boundless. (2022). World history 1: Ancient civilizations – enlightenment - Version 35. Retrieved from https://archive.org/details/boundless-world-history/boundless-world-history/page/n983/mode/2up

Britannica. (n.d.). Roman adoption of Hellenistic education. Retrieved from https://www.britannica.com/topic/education/Roman-adoption-of-Hellenistic-education

Cartledge, P. (2016, June 3). Ancient Greeks would not recognize our 'democracy' - they'd see an 'oligarchy'. The

Conversation. Retrieved from https://theconversation.com/ancient-greeks-would-not-recognise-our-democracy-theyd-see-an-oligarchy-60277

Coco, A. A. (2019). Cause, course, and consequence: The Punic wars (264 BCE to 146 BCE) (Publication no. 645) [Honors thesis, Wellesley College]. Wellesley College Digital Repository. Retrieved from https://repository.wellesley.edu/object/ir894?utm_source=repository.wellesley.edu/thesiscollection/645&utm_medium=PDF&utm_campaign=PDFCoverPages

Curry, A. (2021, September 24). They may have founded Rome, then vanished. New work sheds light on the mysterious Etruscans. Science. Retrieved from https://www.science.org/content/article/they-may-have-founded-rome-then-vanished-work-sheds-light-mysterious-etruscans

DailyHistory.org. (n.d.). How did the Etruscans shape Roman history and society? Retrieved from https://dailyhistory.org/How_did_the_Etruscans_shape_Roman_history_and_society

Dillon, M. (2019, June 25). Gods in Ancient Greece and Rome. In Oxford Research Encyclopedia of Religion.

Retrieved from https://oxfordre.com/religion/display/10.1093/acrefore/9780199340378.001.0001/acrefore-9780199340378-e-104

Gokhale, A. P. (2021, September 5). The Contribution of Ancient Greek culture to Modern Age. Countercurrents.org. Retrieved from https://countercurrents.org/2021/09/the-contribution-of-ancient-greek-culture-to-the-modern-age/

Grant, M. (2022, August 9). Roman religion. In Encyclopedia Britannica. Retrieved from https://www.britannica.com/topic/Roman-religion

Immacolata, E. (2015). Syrian Wars. In Y. Le Bohec (Ed.), Wiley Online Library. John Wiley & Sons. Retrieved from https://onlinelibrary.wiley.com/doi/10.1002/9781118318140.wbra1469

Jones, M. (2022, July 27). Greek philosophy: A unique culture that helped build the modern world. Library for Kids. Retrieved from https://libraryforkids.com/greek-philosophy-a-unique-culture-that-helped-build-the-modern-world/

Owlcation. (2022, September 9). 11 ways ancient Greece influenced modern society. Retrieved from https://owlcation.com/humanities/Greek-Influences-today

Tschierse, K. (2022, April 19). Thank you, Roman spirit of innovation! DW. Retrieved from https://www.dw.com/en/roman-inventions-that-influence-our-lives-today/a-61499759

UNRV Roman History. (n.d.). The first Macedonian war. Retrieved from https://www.unrv.com/empire/first-macedonian-war.php

Wasson, D. L. (2016, October 24). Roman Egypt. In World History Encyclopedia. Retrieved from https://www.worldhistory.org/Roman_Egypt/

www.ingramcontent.com/pod-product-compliance
Lightning Source LLC
LaVergne TN
LVHW012247070526
838201LV00090B/143